BREAKING FREE

FROM A

NEGATIVE SELF-IMAGE

D1708483

Charisma HOUSE
A STRANG COMPANY

LINDA MINTLE, PH.D.

BREAKING FREE FROM A NEGATIVE SELF-IMAGE by
Linda S. Mintle, Ph.D.
Published by Charisma House
A Strang Company
600 Rinehart Road
Lake Mary, Florida 32746
www.charismahouse.com

Cover design by Debbie Lewis
Interior design by David Bilby

Library of Congress Catalog Card Number: 2002108793

International Standard Book Number: 0-88419-894-4

This book is not intended to provide therapy, counseling, clinical advice or treatment or to take the place of clinical advice and treatment from your personal physician or professional mental health provider. Readers are advised to consult their own qualified healthcare physicians regarding mental health and medical issues. Neither the publisher nor the author takes any responsibility for any possible consequences from any treatment, action or application of information in this book to any reader. Names, places and identifying details with regard to stories in this book have been changed to protect the privacy of individuals who may have had similar experiences. The people referenced consist of composites of a number of people with similar issues, and the names and circumstances have been changed to protect their confidentiality. Any similarity between the names and stories of individuals described in this book to individuals known to readers is purely coincidental.

04 05 06 07 08 — 10 9 8 7 6 5 4 3
Printed in the United States of America

God does not love us because we are valuable; we are valuable because God loves us.

—Martin Luther

Contents

"I deserve to be punished."

"I'm really GROSS. *No one ever asks me out."*

"I hate it when I make a mistake."

"I hate those women in the magazines. I feel so *u g l y*."

"The teacher said I'll never make anything out of my life."

"I'LL NEVER SUCCEED."

"If only I were thinner..."

"My life is a WASTE."

"I don't know who I am or what I want."

"If only I could be more successful."

"When I look in the mirror, **I hate what I see!"**

INTRODUCTION

Sound familiar? I could go on. The list of negative self-statements is endless. Do you constantly put yourself down? Are you always thinking of ways to impress others? Can you accept a compliment? Are you dissatisfied with your body? Do you wish you were someone else? Do you brag to cover up insecurity? Do you secretly hate yourself?

Or are you proud of the fact that you love yourself? Armed with self-help books, tapes, seminars and workshops, you've practiced the gospel of self-affirmation. You've swallowed the lie that if you just feel better about yourself, everything else will fall into place. But it hasn't, and your self-image remains vulnerable to what people say and what you perceive. Under that façade of self-confidence is deep insecurity.

If you found yourself in either of these extreme descriptions, your self-image is distorted.

Because we are created in the image of God, a healthy self-image apart from Him is impossible. And yet we are deceived into thinking it can be done. In today's world, we are told over and over to deify, glamorize, beautify and pamper the self. "Love yourself." "Be good to yourself." "Affirm yourself." "You determine your destiny." "Trust your heart." "There is great power within you." "Your life is what you make of it." "You deserve the best." What results from all this self-focus is not a positive self-image but self-love or narcissism.

Our image is not rooted in the self *at all. We are beautiful reflections of God, His handiwork and design.*

The truth? Our image is not rooted in the *self* at all. We are beautiful reflections of God, His handiwork and design. The problem is we *don't* see ourselves in His light. That's why I'm writing this book. We often fail to understand who we are in Christ and search for affirmation from all the wrong sources.

Can You Relate?

Do you remember actress Sally Field's Academy Award acceptance speech in which she gushed to the audience, "You like me. You really like me"? Here was an accomplished woman with major talent focusing on being liked by her unseen public! Negative self-image is epidemic. And it's a serious problem because it blocks us from intimacy with God. God doesn't want you because you have a beautiful exterior, an impressive résumé or because you're famous. He wants you.

Ellen

Ellen stared out the window. "This wasn't the way it was supposed to be. I went to college, chose a career, made some money and married a great guy. I live well. We have all the toys—you know, the BMW, SUV, the Bang & Olufsen sound system, the boat docked at the lake, the summer condo in the mountains with the new European kitchen. But my life is on cruise control.

"Steve, my husband, is wildly successful

with his advertising agency. I have a great interior design business. I'm busy but restless. I'm living the life most people dream of, and yet, something is missing. Even with all this 'stuff,' I don't like myself very well. Everything I am is wrapped up in what I do or what I have. After September 11, it all seems meaningless."

Looking at Ellen you would never guess that this tall, dark and beautiful woman could feel such insecurity. By appearances, she had it all—the complete package—good looks, a successful husband, two darling children and the life of luxury. These things, however, failed to define or satisfy her. And her negative self-image loomed despite all her success.

Chris

Chris sat with his arms crossed. "I don't like to talk about myself. I mean, what's the point? I've screwed up so many times. God…who's He? I'm too messed up for God. My entire life has been about partying and feeling good. Yeah, it's pretty empty, but I don't really care anymore. I know I'm a screwup. If I don't care, why should God?

"I've been teased most of my life. People make fun of my body. I'm not very athletic, and I'm bad at sports. I never really fit in. At first it hurt to be so out of the 'in group.' Eventually, I just stopped caring. Well, actually, I just stopped feeling. I guess the partying kind of makes me forget."

Samantha

"Sounds crazy, but I don't even want to date. I hate myself. Why would any man be attracted to me? What do I have to offer anyone? I'm so ordinary it hurts. The plain-Jane who just isn't outstanding at anything. My sister, on the other hand, is beautiful and talented. It seems so totally unfair. I feel depressed.

"It's easier to be anonymous. When I was in high school I had awful acne. I grew my hair long so it would sort of cover my face. You know…I could hide. People knew me as 'the quiet one,' but they didn't really know how much I wanted friends. I keep wondering how different my life might be if I could just develop some confidence. Mostly, I just want to avoid people. It's easier but lonely."

Jared

"Men are supposed to look buff. I've been working out now for three years; if I miss a day, I really worry about it. I go to the gym no matter how busy I am. My girlfriend says I'm obsessed. She claims I love the workouts more than spending time with her. You know, I do love the feeling I get when pumping iron. I feel strong and in control, not something I feel when I'm dealing with relationships. Relationships are a pain.

"Lately, though, I've been concerned. I'm getting into stacking, and even though I know it's potentially addictive, I'm seeing fantastic results! People keep noticing I've been working out; only makes me want to do it more. No matter what people say, I'm still nowhere near what I could be."

These people are not alone in their struggles to find and/or accept who they are. In their minds, they don't measure up. Somehow they "know" something is missing or feel as if they aren't quite good enough. Whether it's physical attraction, athletic ability, intelligence, success or some other self-imposed measurement, they fall short. As a result, too much of their daily life is negatively affected by these distortions.

Since few of us have the ideal figure or the perfect life, why do we give so much time and energy to attaining both? Look around. Daily, we fight a culture that reinforces these unrealistic ideals and focuses on the *external*. And it seems that regardless of the cost, we are willing to pay it.

It's time to break free from negative self-image and learn how to be esteemed from the true source.

But can all this self-obsession bring us true happiness and contentment? Can we develop a view of ourselves that is accepting? And is the pursuit of a highly regarded self-image even biblical? It's time to break free from negative self-image and learn how to be esteemed from the true source. In this book you will:

- Understand how negative self-image develops.
- Approach the notion of self-image from a biblical basis.

- Identify who you are in Christ.
- Use break-free strategies to change your image and behavior.
- Learn to live as a reflection of God's image.

Whether you hate yourself, wish you could be different, sometimes struggle with negative self-image, fight negative thoughts or overevaluate your importance, this book will give you a godly context from which to see yourself.

BREAKING FREE

PRAYER FOR YOU

Lord, whether I think of myself more highly than I should or loathe the creation You made, help me to ground my thinking in You and not the world around me. I want to be free from this negative self-image bondage.

Chapter 1

Understanding Negative Self-Image

Most people are other people. Their thoughts are someone else's opinions, their lives a mimicry, their passions a quotation.

—Oscar Wilde

Houston, we have a problem!

A recent survey of fifth- through twelfth-grade girls may shock you:

- 59 percent were dissatisfied with their bodies (29 percent were actually overweight).
- 66 percent wanted to lose weight.
- 47 percent reported that looking in fashion magazines made them want to lose weight *now*.

- 69 percent said the fashion magazine pictures influenced their view of the ideal body.[1]

Why are these statistics so important? They reflect a growing concern. More girls and boys report dissatisfaction with their bodies at young ages. And negative body image is often associated with substance abuse, eating disorders and other mental health conditions.

It's Greek to Me!

Our cultural obsession with looks and beauty is reflected in the story of the Greek mythology character Narcissus. The story goes like this: Echo, the beautiful wood nymph, finds Narcissus highly attractive and desperately seeks his attention, only to be shunned. Others are also taken by his beauty, but Narcissus does not return their admiration. After a certain maiden is rebuffed, she prays for Narcissus to experience love that is not returned. An avenging goddess grants her prayer, and Narcissus falls in love with his reflection in a pool of water. Obsessed with his image, he pines away until he finally disappears, and in his place a flower grows.

You don't have to understand rocket science to get the point. Self-love takes you down a path of destruction and will not satisfy your deepest longing. You weren't designed for self-love, but for a love much greater.

So what is negative self-image? Simply put, it's the negative view you hold of yourself—how you think and talk about yourself. Self-esteem, self-worth, self-regard and self-assurance are all related concepts. Negative self-image develops, in part, from feedback we experience from others. If the voices around us are negative, we tend to internalize that feedback and make it our own.

Self-love takes you down a path of destruction and will not satisfy your deepest longing.

In addition, we self talk. Our internal conversations or automatic thoughts conclude we are somehow inadequate. When self-talk or self-evaluation is overly critical, negative, hateful, loathing, arrogant or prideful, it affects our behavior. For example, someone who hates her body may avoid being with others; a man who constantly thinks of himself as inferior may overcompensate by trying to control others; someone who believes she is worthless may become depressed; a boy who thinks he is superior may bully other kids.

Personal evaluation is always distorted to some degree because we don't see ourselves clearly. We need the Holy Spirit and the Word of God to speak truth to us and make us aware of our shortcomings—not so we can feel bad, but so we can correct distortions.

The development of the self takes place in the context of others. We are relational. As we grow and experience life, we form an identity based on interaction with other people, events and circumstances.

For the Christian, our identity—who we are—is rooted in Christ Jesus. As we die to self, we live and breathe in Him. Apart from Him, we are restless. Self-actualization will bring us no satisfaction.

The Developing Self

Over the years, psychologists have postulated various theories for the developing "self." For example, Freud speaks of drives that must be fulfilled, Maslow of a hierarchy of needs, Rogers of unconditional positive regard, Fromm of the need for self-love, Bowlby of the importance of early experience with attachment figures, Bandura of self-efficacy and so on. Because these theories are typically rooted in the humanistic view that man is ultimately "good," the developing *self* is usually trying to attain "goodness." The mantra of the modern secular world is "love yourself." The belief is that self-love will satisfy the soul and correct a number of social and personal ills along the way.

Young children base their developing sense of self on feelings of love, acceptance and being valued by significant others. In the first few years of life, love and acceptance usually set the stage for later feelings of self-esteem. Along with being valued and accepted, parental love must include realistic expectations, limits and controls.

Experiences that provide meaningful challenges and opportunities for effort assist the healthy developing self.[2]

But what about those children who are not valued or loved unconditionally? According to object relations theorists, the quality of early parental (mostly the mother) attachment helps or hinders a child in later life. If a child is not valued or comforted, he/she may feel worthless and of little value. These feelings of worthlessness then reinforce the belief that one is of little value. This *belief* gets translated into *behavior* (such as low social competence and lack of success in school), which reinforces the feelings of low self-esteem, and so the cycle goes.

BREAKING FREE

MENTAL HEALTH FACT

Family—and Me

Family relationships are also powerful influencers of how we view ourselves. I've counseled numerous people from families where their physical appearance was constantly made fun of, degraded or violated—fathers who negatively comment on their daughter's weight or looks; mothers who obsess on weight or body image and model negative comments toward the self; parents who are depressed, addicted and unable to function; siblings who cruelly poke fun and engage in regular put-downs; abuse that violates or attempts to obliterate the self; relatives who make rude comments that go unchecked. It all adds up to negative self-image.

If you think about it, adults who have difficulty accepting God's unconditional love usually come from families in which parental love was conditional, abusive or absent. Performance was emphasized or neglect of emotional needs was paramount. Success and outward appearance were highly valued. Children learned they were loved based on what they did, what they achieved or how they looked, or they weren't accepted at all.

For a child, parents are the earthly models for imaging Christ.

For a child, parents are the earthly models for imaging Christ. If those images are negative or absent, the love of God is hard to grasp. When children are uncertain of love, either because it is absent, conditional, abusive or overly permissive, problems with image arise.

As children grow, they interact with the larger society, which also influences the development of self-image. Americans tend to emphasize physical appearance, physical ability, achievement, peer acceptance and a number of personal traits as criteria for healthy self-esteem.[3] Independence is highly valued. The self is validated through individual achievements as we compare ourselves to others.

Our standards for beauty are depicted through media. Open any magazine, spend just a few seconds watching music videos, see a movie or watch television, especially the advertisements. All of these media reflect someone's idea of the perfectly attractive, successful, desirable person. Bombarded with these images over time, we eventually begin to believe that this is how we are to look and what we need to be happy.

Competitive achievement is also highly valued in America. Winning means someone else loses, and the losers are left to feel inadequate or inferior. Negative feelings become more prevalent as children lose the competitive races of life or struggle to find their personal success.

Others simply identify with winners in an attempt to raise feelings of self-esteem. This "reflected glory" comes when you associate with a winner or successful group and distance yourself from losers.[4] Think about our national obsession with designer clothes or sports, for example. As a fan of the Chicago Bulls (back when they had Michael Jordan and were winning), I basked in the glory of their success and took pride that my hometown was home of the World Champions! As a fan, I did nothing to contribute to their on-court success, but I certainly could reflect it. Being a Bulls' fan was somehow self-enhancing (not anymore!).

Teachers, bosses and friends all have a voice in the way we see ourselves. These voices can be positive or negative. I've counseled many who were told by a teacher that they'd never make it through school. Others had special coaches, teachers, a big brother, a grandparent or someone who encouraged them to achieve.

Gender influences self-image. In America, girls in the dominant white culture are expected to be beautiful and thin. The pressure to look a certain way is enormous and plays a role in the development of body image distortion and eating disorders. More recently, boys have begun to feel the pressure as they buy into the media's masculine, athletic ideal.

Race and ethnicity play a role in developing self-image. For example, African American women as a cultural group seem to have fewer body image distortions than whites.[5] The thinking is that both groups of women partially base their physical body judgments on what men of their race desire. African American women believe that African American males prefer larger women, and white women believe that white men prefer ultra-thin women.

Consequently, white women have more body image distortion.

Of course, not all women within ethnic or racial categories are the same. In the case noted above, African American women who more strongly identify with the dominant white culture are more at risk for body image distortion and eating disorders than those who don't.[6]

For years educators have promoted the idea that a positive self-image will help children learn. Yet untold thousands of dollars later, the research doesn't support such a conclusion. Feeling good about themselves doesn't make children perform better in school.[7]

Low self-esteem is often cited as a cause for crime, violence and other antisocial acts. This too is misguided. Criminals, gang members and bullies often have inflated views of self and will attack anyone who challenges their self-image. In fact, high self-esteem is often related to aggression.[8]

Different cultures have different ideas about the self. For example, Eastern cultures define the self in a much more social context. The *inter*dependent self is able to adjust to others and maintain harmony. Self-restraint is valued along with modesty and connectedness with others. Taking pride in one's accomplishments is seen as gloating and is not acceptable.[9] Positive feelings come from doing things that help others. Easterners define "self" in a very un-American way.

Furthermore, low self-esteem has been linked to all kinds of social and personal problems not borne out by research. In America, there is a premium on feeling good about ourselves. We've allowed opinions, experiences, people and our perceptions to define us. In so doing we conclude that we are inferior, a loser, weak and inadequate, untalented, unable to compete and unattractive because we compare ourselves to others. We listen to the voices of significant others and then allow the culture to dictate our values.

We are created in the image of Someone and designed to communicate with Him.

We forget the radical words of Jesus.

We are not just body, but soul and spirit. We are created in the image of Someone and designed to communicate with Him. And no matter what our circumstances or life experiences, we can be free of negative self-image because of Christ.

The Emotional Toll

It's that dreaded moment. You slip off your shoes (that's at least two pounds), your jacket (another pound), your watch (few ounces) and step on the scales. You don't want to look because you know you're retaining water. Besides, the doctor's scales are always off a good five pounds. Then, the nurse loudly announces the number as if it's no big deal. You wish it weren't, but it is! And does she have to say it so loudly?

No matter how emotionally healthy we are, we still obsess about our weight. What woman doesn't want to lose another five pounds? How many of us lie about weight on our driver's license? Weight matters, especially to women. In fact, most of us think we are too fat.

Few of us look like the *Sports Illustrated* swimsuit models, yet we spend billions of dollars on weight loss products and magical cures for obesity. Why are we so consumed with dieting? We've allowed the media to dictate body image. The constant images of glamour and beauty—TV, movies, magazines, music videos and advertisements—take a toll. Even when standing in the grocery store line, we can't avoid the tabloids promising to melt the fat like wax from our thighs.

With all our emphasis on thinness, 54 percent of Americans are overweight.[10] Approximately 11 million suffer from eating disorders.[11] The average American woman is five feet four inches tall, 144 pounds and a size twelve. Compare that to the average model, five feet eight inches tall, 110 pounds and a size two. Take a look at that glamorous air-brushed model pictured in the magazine, then look in the mirror. It's easy to be depressed.

The cultural pressure to be thin is so intense that nine-year-old girls are dieting and teen plastic surgery is on the rise.

Billions of dollars are spent on shaping, cutting, stapling and lopping off parts of the female body. In America, women, more so than men, define themselves by their bodies. Typically we don't like what we see.

It is also estimated that about one in fifty suffers from body dysmorphic disorder (BDD), an unclassified disorder characterized by excessive concern about one's appearance, body shape, body size, weight, perceived lack of muscles, facial blemishes, hair and so forth. The preoccupation with appearance is imagined or based on a slight flaw, most often concerning hair, nose or skin.[12] In some cases this disorder leads to steroid abuse, unnecessary plastic surgery and depression. It occurs frequently in teens and twenty-year-olds who tend to be perfectionists.

Negative self-image creates emotional bondage. The pressure to look good at any cost is enormous. Appearance is everything. Pretense is paramount. People can't see the real you. They might not like her. So don't expose your weaknesses. Live your life projecting a false image. The problem is that all this dishonesty is exhausting. It requires constant energy to maintain perfection. And it is easy to feel out of control because of the power others have been given to determine your worth on any given day.

Maybe you respond to image problems with false humility and hide from responsibility. "I can't possibly do anything for God. I'm not anyone important. I have no talents. I'm OK hugging my pew and living a good life for God. Don't push me to do anything I'm not comfortable doing. I prefer to observe. There are plenty of others whom God has called and is using in a great way. He doesn't need me."

You are here for a purpose and have a divine destiny.

This, of course, is nonsense! As clichéd as it sounds, you are here for a purpose and have a divine destiny. Failure to recognize this keeps you emotionally bound. False humility is as destructive as pride. It condemns and immobilizes. It blocks you from moving forward to all God has for you.

The results of negative self-image are far

reaching. Relationships with others and God are affected. So too are emotional well-being, school and vocational achievements, behavior and the quality of our communication and problem-solving.

So how are we to think of ourselves? Do we try to impress others? Do we create another "person" we like better? Are we trying to be "real" but don't know what that is? The answers are found in what God has to say about us.

BREAKING FREE

PRAYER FOR YOU

Lord, I see myself in such a negative light. I have been influenced by so many things and people. Somehow, I have ignored what You have to say about me. Forgive me for giving power to others to determine who I am. I want to be free of this bondage. Help me to see the truth by searching Your Word.

CHAPTER 2

GOD ESTEEM

No sooner do we believe that God loves us than there is an impulse to believe that He does so, not because He is Love, but because we are intrinsically lovable.

—C. S. LEWIS

Negative self-image is corrected through a proper understanding of the basis of esteem. The *path* you take to develop a healthy image is important. If you try to love yourself without understanding who you are in Christ, you will fail. Esteem does not come from inside you, other people, your family or accomplishments. You are highly esteemed because God created and chose you. This very simple truth is often difficult to grasp because it is so countercultural.

All the modern emphasis on increasing self-love has not resulted in the desired effects. Self-love does not improve personal and social ills the way we hoped it would. In fact, it often has the opposite effect—it creates arrogant, self-centered people who are out for themselves, obsessed with body image and the accumulation of things, or aggressive children who defend their images at any cost.

The transforming message of Jesus was not about self-love. His energy was not spent trying to get people to feel better about themselves. In fact, Paul warns us not to think more highly of ourselves than we should (Rom. 12:3); not to boast or compare ourselves with others (2 Cor. 10:12); and to acknowledge that we already have a tendency to love our own flesh (Eph. 5:29). So self-love isn't the path to a happier or more fulfilled life.

The message of Christ was about sacrificial love. As He walked the earth, He loved, served, empowered and laid down His life for others. His command to us was love *God* and *others*. When asked by the scribes which command was the greatest of all, Jesus replied:

> The first of all the commandments is: "Hear, O Israel, the LORD our God, the LORD is one. And you shall love the LORD your God with all your heart, with all your soul, with all your mind, and with all your strength." This is the first commandment. And the second, like it, is this: "You shall love your neighbor as yourself." There is no other commandment greater than these.
>
> —MARK 12:29–31, NKJV

As we allow the love of God to flood us, we change. Love is the key to a healthy self-image. *Not self-love, but accepting God's love.*

Our Creator knows we have a tendency toward sin—worshiping other things, images or people and placing importance on the insignificant. But the Scriptures tell us that God doesn't look on outward appearances, rather on the heart.

Love is the key to a healthy self-image. Not self-love, but accepting God's love.

> But the LORD said to Samuel, "Do not consider his *appearance* or his height, for I have rejected him. The LORD does not look at the things man looks at. Man looks at the outward appearance, but the LORD looks at the heart."
>
> —1 SAMUEL 16:7, EMPHASIS ADDED

WHOSE IMAGE DO WE REFLECT—GOD'S OR MAN'S?

Genesis 1:26–27 reports, "Then God said, 'Let us make man in our *image*, in our likeness, and let them rule over the fish of the sea and the birds of the air, over the livestock, over all the earth, and over all the creatures that move along the ground.' So God created man in his own *image*, in the *image* of God he created him; male and female he created them" (emphasis added). Again we are reminded in Genesis 9:6, "Whoever sheds the blood of man, by man shall his blood be shed; for in the *image* of God has God made man" (emphasis added). Clearly, God created us in His image.

This is pretty clear. We are the reflected image of God. And it is God's desire that we accurately mirror His glory. In the New

Testament, Paul again reminds us that we are the image and glory of God (1 Cor. 11:7). He tells us that those who don't know Christ are blinded to this fact. "The god of this age has blinded the minds of unbelievers, so that they cannot see the light of the gospel of the glory of Christ, who is the *image* of God" (2 Cor. 4:4, emphasis added).

God wants us to have a healthy view of ourselves. He doesn't want us engaged in self-loathing, false humility or pride.

Furthermore, it is God's desire that we fashion our image after Christ, who is the image of the invisible God (Col. 1:15). The more we imitate Him, the more we reproduce His glory "...and have put on the new self, which is being renewed in knowledge in the image of its Creator" (Col. 3:10).

God wants us to have a healthy view of ourselves. He doesn't want us engaged in self-loathing, false humility or pride.

So how do we correct our distorted view?

First, consider Creation. We are God's

design, which He declared, “Good.” His decision to create us, in His image, had nothing to do with us! We are His idea!

After we became so deceived, He sent Jesus to save us. Jesus charges us to imitate Him.

BREAKING FREE

MENTAL HEALTH FACT

Imitate Jesus

According to the Bible, Jesus:

- Was charismatic
- Was excitable
- Was moved with compassion
- Was filled with emotion
- Was passionate
- Was adventurous
- Was bold
- Was honest
- Praised other people
- Was intimate
- Was sensitive to women
- Was patient
- Was ready to help
- Was a master teacher who taught with full authority
- Was full of grace and truth

- Was without sin
- Was fearless
- Refused coercive power
- Was humble
- Was a servant to others
- Possessed little
- Was merciful
- Hated pride

Jesus' deeds, thoughts and character are recorded, not His physical appearance. It is obvious: Jesus wants our hearts, not our bodies.

In order to change our view of self, we need to change our thinking. Our accomplishments, appearance or good deeds do not make us acceptable to God. The way to a healthy image is to love God and allow His love to be seen in you. Let's start at the beginning.

Should Anything Be Above God?

In Leviticus 26:1 we read, "Do not make idols or set up an image or a sacred stone for yourselves, and do not place a carved stone in your land to bow down before it. I am the LORD your God." In Deuteronomy 27:15, God adds, "'Cursed is the man who carves an image or casts an idol—a thing detestable to the LORD, the work of the craftsman's hands—and sets it up in secret.' Then all the people shall say, 'Amen!'" Psalm 97:7 adds, "All who worship images are put to shame, those who boast in idols—worship him, all you gods!"

Typically we think of worshiping images as bowing to statues or worshiping the sun or some other object. But when you obsess on the *self*, it too can become an idol. Anything and everything pursued for the purpose of self-worth can take on idol proportion. Whether it's attaining the best clothes, the most expensive car, the biggest house, the perfect body or anything else, we must be careful not to love or worship these things. Nor should we look to these things to define us.

The bottom line is that we are made in God's image.

Here are additional scriptures that help us to understand how to think about ourselves in relationship with God.

MENTAL HEALTH FACT

God and Us

1. *Nothing can compare with God—Isaiah 40:18:* "To whom, then, will you compare God? What image will you compare him to?" There is nothing that will satisfy your longing to be loved but God. Stop looking elsewhere.

2. *Our natural inclination is to love ourselves—Ephesians 5:29–30:* "After all, no one ever hated his own body, but he feeds and cares for it, just as Christ does the church—for we are members of his body."

3. *We are predestined to be conformed to His image—Romans 8:29:* "For those God foreknew he also predestined to be conformed to the likeness of his Son, that he might be the firstborn among many brothers."

   Psalm 139:13–16: "For you created my inmost being; you knit me together in my mother's womb. I praise you because I am fearfully and wonderfully made; your works are wonderful, I know that full well. My frame was not hidden from you when I was made in the secret place. When I was woven together in the depths of the earth, your eyes saw my unformed body."

4. *He transforms us to His image—2 Corinthians 3:18:* "And we, who with unveiled faces all reflect the Lord's glory, are being transformed into his likeness with ever-increasing glory, which comes from the Lord, who is the Spirit."

5. *The goal is less of me and more of Him—John 3:30:* "He must become greater; I must become less."

6. *We are warned against pride and self-love—Romans 12:3:* "For by the grace given me I say to every one of you: Do not think of yourself more highly than you ought, but rather think of yourself with sober judgment, in accordance with the measure of faith God has given you."

7. *God deals with us individually, so don't compare—2 Corinthians 10:12–17:* "We do not dare to classify or compare ourselves with some who commend themselves. When they measure themselves by themselves and compare themselves with themselves, they are not wise. We, however, will not boast beyond proper limits, but will confine our boasting to the field God has assigned to us, a field that reaches even to you. We are not going too far in our boasting, as would be the case if we had not come to you, for we did get as far as you with the gospel of Christ. Neither do we go beyond our limits by boasting of work done by others. Our hope is that, as your faith continues to grow, our area of activity among you will greatly expand, so that we can preach the gospel in the regions beyond you. For we do not want to boast about work already done in another man's territory. But, '*Let him who boasts boast in the Lord*'" (emphasis added).

8. *We can rid ourselves of negative self-image—Hebrews 12:1:* "Therefore, since we are surrounded by such a great cloud of witnesses, *let us throw off everything that hinders and the sin that so easily entangles*, and let us run with perseverance the race marked out for us" (emphasis added). Notice that *we* are told to throw off everything that hinders. This implies initiative and action on our part.

The bottom line is that we are made in God's image. Our esteem comes as a result of knowing Him and His love. As we know Him intimately, He changes us. Nothing we do or have will make us acceptable to God. He unconditionally loves and accepts us. As a good father, He has established guidelines for living and blessing. God esteems us, and we no longer depend on others to define us.

PRAYER FOR YOU

Lord, I accept Your love and believe that I am not a mistake, but created for Your delight. There are no conditions on Your love. As I get to know You, let me reflect Your glory and not man's.

CHAPTER 3

WHO AM I?

If I am what I have, and I lose what I have, who am I?

—FRITZ PERLS

I see a number of young women in therapy who are confused about their identities. As they struggle to make sense of hurtful relationships, they lose a sense of who they are—or perhaps they never knew in the first place. Liz was one of those women.

It was 10:00 A.M. on Tuesday. Time for her appointment. Liz, a petite, fragile-looking blond was one of my "regulars." It was hard for Liz to trust anyone. She had been hurt too many times. Dating was a nightmare. Every school break Liz reappeared on my couch to update me on the latest male who used, abused and left her.

Family life was no picnic, either. Dad, a pushy and successful salesman, drank nightly. He never had much to say, and Liz longed for a relationship with him. Of all the family members, though he seemed the most approachable, he wasn't.

Liz's mom was constantly depressed. The pain in her life was obvious, but she wouldn't talk about it. So Liz spent her days at home distant from a father she desperately longed for and care-taking a mother whose weakness frightened her. One night she met Yvonne.

Yvonne and Liz began to drink together. The drunker they got, the more Liz poured out her heart. "Men are distant. They're no good. I just can't trust them; they're so emotionally stupid and hurtful and powerful. All they want is sex, but then they leave you broken-hearted and empty." Her anger turned to gut-wrenching sobs, and Yvonne was there to comfort. She put her arm around Liz and tenderly kissed her. Liz was shocked, but somehow it felt good. As Yvonne pursued her physically, Liz responded until she found herself sexually involved.

"How could this happen?" she wondered. "Am I gay and just didn't know it?" She felt terrible, but Yvonne's calm reassurances helped. The relationship continued and became more intimate. All Liz could think about was being with Yvonne. Yvonne understood her and knew how to meet her emotional needs. But Liz was confused. She didn't feel attracted to other women and didn't think she was gay, yet she was having a gay relationship. Over time, Yvonne felt suffocated by Liz's neediness and eventually broke off the relationship. Liz was devastated and depressed. What was happening, and what did it all mean in terms of her identity?

Liz's attraction to Yvonne did not stem from deep-seated lesbian feelings. Yvonne represented a strong, nurturing woman who paid attention to Liz and met her needs. All of these things were missing in Liz's development. Because of the lack of family intimacy and the years of rejection with men, Liz was susceptible to Yvonne's advances. Yvonne, she thought, could meet all her needs and be the solution to all her pain.

Possessing little esteem, feeling bitter toward men and upset with her family's lack of attention and nurturance, Liz was ripe for emotional picking. Confusing sex with love, the emotional ties to Yvonne intensified a strong dependency. From Yvonne she thought she would gain self-worth and acceptance. She yearned for love to be returned. When the relationship ended, Liz was a mess.

Liz looked for her identity and security in another woman. The lie she believed was that a woman could love her and meet all her needs. After Yvonne broke off the relationship, Liz fell into despair. Men hurt her, and now women did, too. No one could give her what she needed. Liz didn't know that her yearning for love was meant to be filled by God.

As an adult woman, Liz had to recognize the shortcomings of her parents and stop waiting for them to embrace her need for intimacy. The hurt she experienced from men created deep wounds. Through that wounding, she was deceived, thinking only strong women were safe. Ultimately, Liz learned that only God could fill the empty places and keep her from developing unhealthy dependencies on others.

Although you may not have experienced the same hurts Liz did, your quest for self-identity can be equally challenging.

In order to break free from a negative self-image, you must identify with God. You are, as apologist Os Guinness writes in his book *The Call*, called to Someone.[1] There is a purpose and divine plan for your life. Discovering both is only possible through relationship with God. Your identity is found in Him.

The process of building a godly identity often requires a renewing of the mind.

In order to build a strong foundation for esteem and image, knowing your identity is essential. It must begin with basic truths.

The process of building a godly identity often requires a renewing of the mind. The Word of God may counter the words you have heard all your life. Maybe you've been told you are worthless or won't amount to anything. Or maybe you feel failed or unattractive. Whatever the case, the correction requires that you change your distorted view.

WHAT DO YOU BELIEVE?

Think about it for a moment, because your first response may be to answer what you *know*. You may *know* lots of Bible facts and Sunday school stories. Hopefully you know that Jesus died on the cross to save you from your sins and that He rose again. And with the popularity of the Left Behind series, you know He is coming back. These things you *know*.

But what do you *believe*? Listen to what my good friend and now author James Langteaux says about believing in his book *God.com*.

BREAKING FREE

MENTAL HEALTH FACT

Believing Is...

We are all dying to believe. And dying because we don't. I think believing is a little like looking past what we can see into the eyes of God while falling

> forward into the blackness—forward, ever forward—free-falling until finally we can see. When we do, what we see is what HE sees. But only after becoming His pupil...Being interactive with the God of the universe requires the simple belief that He is willing and able to speak to us, to become involved in our daily lives, to care enough to send us the very best.[2]

Do you believe that you can have a daily, interactive relationship with the living God? Do you believe Jesus' words in John 14:12: "He who believes in Me, the works that I do, he will do also; and greater works than these he will do because I go to My Father" (NKJV). Have you done great works for God because you believe? If you believe, then you must *get to know* your Father. There are many who believe God exists but don't know Him. It is through relationship with God that you will be transformed.

Distortions of God

Our families are basic sources of learning,

but they can also be sources of distortion when it comes to understanding the character of God. Families are supposed to love unconditionally. They are supposed to protect us and never let us down. In reality they often fail us. Then, as in the story of Liz, we look to other people to love us unconditionally. We hope our friends, the church or fellow Christians will show us love, but we are often let down in those relationships as well. When this happens we transfer our views of failed love to God. God gets all the negative attributes and then doesn't look so appealing, either. We look to other sources to answer the age-old question, "Who am I?"

Some of you have dads you don't really know. They may be absent, uninterested, distant, emotionally cut off, self-absorbed, critical, shaming, perfectionists, violent, drunk or even abusive. Others have mothers who suffer depression and anxiety, who may be physically present but emotionally absent or distracted with their own issues. Real intimacy is missing.

Because we tend to transfer our feelings about earthly parents to God the Father, we may not want to know Him. We may prefer to keep distant. Intimacy, as we know it, is too painful.

The search for masculine identity

When I appeared on the *Queen Latifa* show a few years ago to talk about teen violence, several teens were also scheduled as guests on the show. Basically, they wanted to blow up their schools and hurt others or themselves. As I spoke to these kids in the green room before the show, the absence of parental love was very apparent. One was a gang member, another a Goth; others had siblings now jailed for shooting sprees at their local high schools. Even their friends were killers.

Behind the bravado, makeup, hip-hop tattoos and dog collars were hurting kids who had no fathers in their lives. One teen was accompanied by his mom's boyfriend, who was drunk and verbally abusive. The mother was so depressed she could hardly function. No wonder these teens were lost, looking for a place to belong and be loved.

Every boy on that television set was searching for masculine identity. Each one had a father who had abandoned him. Their identities were found with the gangs and loner kids who expressed their hurt through anger and violence. As one teen explained, "Boys don't cry and whine; they get even." As they searched for connection, they found community with other lost souls.

Eating disorders

Eating disorders are symptomatic of failed attempts to develop identity. Esteem and love are sought through attaining the perfect body. Self-sacrifice and self-denial are powerful ways of avoiding accurate self-definition. Through the process of bingeing and purging or self-starvation, girls develop an identity defined by food obsession. It's a painful and abusive way to attain self-definition and independence.

Trying to lose ourselves

There are other ways we lose ourselves so we don't have to face the work of finding ourselves:

- Through drugs, pornography or alcohol
- Through sexual activity

- Through accomplishment, good grades
- Through sports
- Through work and success
- Even through religion

When people feel lost and purposeless, they may look for God. If you ask, many people tell you they believe there is a God. He's out there somewhere, not too involved, way off in the distance—kind of like Bette Midler sang in her hit song.

Making God Who We Want Him to Be

For many of us, God becomes whoever we want Him to be. We fit Him into whatever is convenient for our beliefs. He can be a goddess, nature, a healing presence, any form of higher power...whatever we want to make Him. And in order to be politically correct, we can be tolerant of all forms of God.

One morning I sat in the green room of a CBS television station preparing to do a morning talk show. As usual, there were other guests in the green room. One engaged me in conversation. Somehow, she told me, she'd "intuited" that I was "spiritual." She saw an aura around me.

As we talked, I discovered she did "spiritual readings" for people who patronized a local health store. She explained that she, like me, was a healer. "I'm curious," I asked. "What is the source of your healing power?"

She explained that she did Christ-centered healing. Now my interest was really piqued, so I asked her to tell me more about it. "Christ," she explained, "is one of the angels and is perhaps the greatest. He and His angels are the source of my power."

"Is Christ the Son of God?" I asked.

"Oh no," she replied. "Just an important angel."

When I mentioned my belief that Jesus was the Son of God, she frowned. "That's far too limiting and really characteristic of narrow-minded thinking. Jesus is much more approachable as a good angel."

This woman was searching for God, but she needed to make Him (or her) be who she needed Him to be—powerful, but not too powerful; a healer, but not the Healer.

Christians too have been influenced by this type of thinking. In therapy, for example, Christian teens tell me their sexual activity has nothing to do with their mental health problems. "God is cool, Dr. Mintle. If He knows you love someone, sex is OK. God can deal with it better than you or my parents can!"

My follow-up to this is usually to ask, "I'm curious. You go to church; where did you get that idea?"

"I just know because the minister says God is love. I don't read the Bible—it's too hard to understand and not relevant to my experience. I figure this is the way He is. If He's love, then He's all about love."

These teens are not the only ones ignorant of the Word because they've listened to other people's redefinition of God. Many Christians make God who they want Him to be so they don't have to deal with their behavior. They are without personal, intimate knowledge of God, so He doesn't really impact their lives too much. He's there, conveniently enough, only when they need Him. Frankly, it's hard to identify with a god who appears so nebulous and distant. I know a young man who, although he grew up in a Christian leader's family, has reconstructed God without a Jesus "component." Handy. Now there's no guilt about sin, nor is there need for a savior for his sin. Everybody believes in God. Even Satan.

But *you* have the opportunity to know God if you choose, if you have the desire or interest. In fact, your relationship can become as intimate as you want it. The process of developing intimacy with God is similar to other intimate relationships—you have to spend time with Him (through prayer), get to know Him (through the written Word), listen to what He has to say and then respond by obeying.

When you are in love, it doesn't matter what anyone else says because you are tuned to the voice of your lover. That's how God wants us to be—tuned in and listening to His voice. He's waiting for you to take the necessary steps, to open up, to be vulnerable, to seek Him, to love Him. His love will change you and give you a sense of who you are.

In John 14:9 Jesus said to Philip, "Don't you know me, Philip, even after I have been among you such a long time?" Oswald Chambers explains that these words were not spoken as a rebuke or even with surprise. Jesus is making the point that He seems to be the last one with whom we become intimate. Chambers reminds us that the discipline of life is to enable us to enter into this closest relationship with Jesus Christ. It's not enough to receive His blessing and know His Word. We have to know HIM.[3]

> When once we get intimate with Jesus we are never lonely, we never need sympathy, we can pour out all the time without being pathetic. The saint who is intimate with Jesus will never leave impressions of himself, but only the impression that Jesus is having unhindered way, because the last abyss of his nature has been satisfied by Jesus. The only impression left by such a life is that of the strong calm sanity that only our Lord gives to those who are intimate with Him.[4]

Get to Know Him

Most of us don't know Him, and we don't take the time to get to know Him. Consequently we don't know what He says about us or how He defines us. If we did, we would have no trouble finding our true identity.

If you struggle with a negative self-image and don't know who you are, look to the Bible for answers. It discusses your identity in great detail. If you are saved, you have a family and a place to belong. His words esteem you. A relationship with God corrects the distortions from our human experiences.

On the following pages you will find what God says about your identity. Copy these pages, and keep them with you all the time. Look these verses up in your Bible, and meditate on them. Memorize them as a way to renew your thinking. The enemy wants to keep you bound to a negative self-image. He lies to you about who you are so that you will not move confidently in God's plan for your life. Identify the lies he has spoken to you. Ask God, through His

Word and personal revelation, to bring truth to your thoughts.

Remember: "As a man thinketh, so is he." (See Proverbs 23:7, KJV.)

BREAKING FREE

MENTAL HEALTH FACT

I Am Accepted Because...

Psalm 139:14	I am wonderful. I am fearfully and wonderfully made.
John 1:12	I am God's child.
John 3:16	God loves me just as I am.
John 15:15	As a disciple, I am a friend of Jesus Christ.
Romans 5:1	I have been justified.
1 Corinthians 6:17	I am united with the Lord, and I am one with Him in spirit.
1 Corinthians 6:19–20	I have been bought with a price, and I belong to God.

1 Corinthians 12:27	I am a member of Christ's body.
Ephesians 1:3–8	I have been chosen by God and adopted as His child.
Philippians 4:19	God will supply all my needs.
Colossians 1:13–14	I have been redeemed and forgiven of my sins.
Colossians 2:9–10	I am complete in Christ.
Hebrews 4:14–16	I have direct access to the throne of grace through Jesus Christ.

I Am Secure Because…

Psalm 34:4	I am free from all fears.
Psalm 55:22	God will never allow me to be shaken.
Psalm 56:11	I need not fear any man.
Psalm 91	God rescues and protects me from harm.
Proverbs 28:1	I have the boldness of a lion.

Isaiah 54:17	No weapon formed against me will prosper.
Luke 10:19	I have authority over Satan.
John 8:36	I am free.
John 10:28–30	I am secure in my faith.
Romans 8:1–2	I am free from condemnation.
Romans 8:28	I am assured that God works for my good in all circumstances.
Romans 8:31–39	I am free from any condemnation brought against me and cannot be separated from God's love.
Romans 12:1–2	I need not be squeezed in the world's mold.
2 Corinthians 1:21–22	I have been established, anointed and sealed by God.
Philippians 1:6	I am confident that God will complete the good work He started in me.

Philippians 3:20	I am a citizen of heaven.
Colossians 3:1–4	I am hidden with Christ in God.
2 Timothy 1:7	I have not been given a spirit of fear, but of power, love and a sound mind.
Hebrews 13:5	God will never give up or forsake me.
1 John 5:18	I am born of God, and the evil one cannot touch me.

I Am Significant Because…

Deuteronomy 28:13	I am the head and not the tail. I am above and not beneath.
Psalm 139:2	I am constantly on God's mind.
Psalm 84:11	God will not withhold any good thing from me.
Psalm 37:4	If I delight in God, He will give me my heart's desire.

John 15:5	I am a branch of Jesus Christ, the true vine, and a channel of His life.
John 15:16	I have been chosen and appointed to bear fruit.
1 Corinthians 3:16	I am God's temple.
2 Corinthians 5:17–21	I am a minister of reconciliation for God.
Ephesians 2:6	I am seated with Jesus Christ in the heavenly realm.
Ephesians 2:10	I am God's workmanship.
Ephesians 3:12	I may approach God with freedom and confidence.
Philippians 4:13	I can do all things through Christ, who strengthens me.[5]

When you know who you are in Christ, you no longer worry about image. Others do not have the power to shape your identity. It becomes unnecessary to find your "self" through failed solutions.

Experience God's love. It's not just a feeling, a relationship or an emotion, although we often define love in these ways. His love is an unbreakable promise. It has nothing to do with what you deserve or accomplish. God has a love covenant with you.

God so loved the world that He gave His only Son (John 3:16). Jesus saw us in our dead condition, had compassion on us and was moved to leave heaven and do something for us. Because of His great love for us, He temporarily gave up His place in heaven, surrendered to the will of the Father, came to earth and suffered a horrible death on the cross, just so we could be saved from eternal death. When we were lost, He found us. He had nothing to gain for doing this. His motivation to find us was based on deep compassion. He was willing to give up everything. He made good on His promise. That is authentic love.

Know and *believe* He loves you. Unlike people, God will never let you down. You can depend on His love. You don't deserve such love, but He gives it anyway. Once you understand this and believe it, your life will change. Your esteem and security rest on being loved. No matter what you have done, you are loved.

Perhaps you recall the 1987 Northwest Airlines crash in Detroit, Michigan. All the passengers aboard the flight that day were killed, except one. As the paper reported the gruesome details of smoke, fire and the impact of the crash, it was inconceivable how anyone could survive that flight. But one little four-year-old girl did. Everyone around her lay dead in the hull of the plane. As the emergency crews picked through the rubble of the crash, they found this little girl miraculously alive. How was this possible?

Her mother, knowing the plane was going down and that her child could die, fell to the floor and wrapped her body around the small child. Determined to protect her from death, she covered her like a blanket and refused to let go. Nothing would stop her from loving and protecting that child—not even her own death.

What a vivid picture of how much God

loves you. He has His arms wrapped around you; He wants to protect you and won't ever relax His hold. Even His impending death didn't stop Him from loving you. Let Him hold you close.

To find your true identity, don't look to our culture to define who you are. Surrender all the idols you have unconsciously worshiped. Disconnect from the power sources that surge momentarily but have no transforming power. Sell out. Lose your religion and find intimacy with God.

BREAKING FREE

PRAYER FOR YOU

Lord, I want to know You intimately and to allow Your love to transform me. My identity is in You. Even though I have struggled with knowing who I am, I now know that I am Yours. I am loved. As Your child, my identity is secure. Help me to renew my mind with Your Word, which clearly addresses who I am in You.

CHAPTER 4

BREAK-FREE STRATEGIES: CHANGE YOUR THINKING

A proud mind is high in conceit, self-esteem, and carnal aspiring; a humble mind is high indeed in God esteem, and in holy aspiring.

—MARTIN LUTHER

Now that you understand God's idea of esteem and image and who you are in Christ, continue to renew your mind. The break-free strategies that follow will help change your thoughts, an important step in the process to break free from negative self-image.

Change Your Thinking

1. Let go of past mistakes.

Courtney couldn't get past the abortion she had two years ago. She was a college student who loved to party. Regularly she drank too much and often ended her evenings in bed with someone she barely knew. Courtney got pregnant.

Confused and scared, Courtney had an abortion. As she attempted to resume her life, self-hatred consumed her. Devastated, she turned to God. God forgave her, but Courtney couldn't let go of the guilt. Her head said she was forgiven, but her heart struggled with feeling unloved.

The work to set Courtney free began with letting go of past mistakes and accepting the sacrifice Jesus made on the cross. The blood of Jesus was enough to cover her sins, and she needed to believe it. Because Courtney had never experienced unconditional love, she had trouble believing God could love her with no strings attached. It seemed too good to be true.

Are you tired of feeling judged and condemned for mistakes in your past? Do you regret wasting so much of your life involved with drugs, alcohol and unholy living? Do you have trouble forgiving yourself of an abortion, an affair or acts of immorality? Do you feel bound by the things in your past?

The good news is you don't have to feel this way any longer because the blood of Christ covers past sins. *All* sins. You know Jesus died on the cross to remove your sin, but for some reason, *you* can't get past your mistakes. Consequently, you walk around carrying tremendous guilt and shame.

Guilt is not productive unless it relates to conviction of sin. You *should* feel guilty when you go against God's Word. But once you have repented from sin, you are no longer judged or condemned. Negative self-image can result when you believe God is judging or condemning you, or that what you have done separates you from His love.

Understand this. *Jesus does not accuse you to the Father.* He says so:

> Do not think that I shall accuse you to the Father; there is one who accuses

you—Moses, in whom you trust.

—JOHN 5:45, NKJV

What He is saying here is that we can never measure up to the Law of Moses. All of us sin and fall short of living a perfect life.

Jesus took our failings to the cross where He became the ultimate sacrifice—He became forsaken by God so that He could become the God of the forsaken. We now live under grace, not law. Therefore, when we make mistakes, we are no longer condemned by the old law, but justified through Christ. It's "just as if we'd never sinned." We need to understand this.

The accuser is the devil (Rev. 12:10). He accuses us of failure and inadequacies, of weakness and worthlessness. He lies that we are unworthy of the blood of Jesus. His goal is to penetrate our minds with negativity, which leads to self-destruction. The Bible paints a clear picture of his intentions: "The thief comes only to *steal* and *kill* and *destroy*; I have come that they may have life, and have it to the full" (John 10:10, emphasis added). Satan says you are worthless and hopes you will find self-hate and despair. Christ brings life—you are worthy because of Him. We defeat the accuser by resisting him.

Many of us were taught that the Holy Spirit accuses us of our failings. That teaching was cloaked as "conviction." Remember that Jesus does not accuse us to the Father, and since the Holy Spirit is also part of the Triune God, He won't accuse you, either. He does convict of unbelief (sin) and, instead, brings truth.

This doesn't mean we go on sinning. Sin leads to death. But when we do sin, we need to repent and then know and believe that our sin is gone. When we accept Christ's blood sacrifice, we can't live in condemnation. The cross covered *all* our sin, not just some of it. So drop unhealthy guilt and shame. Jesus does not accuse you. Stop accusing yourself and listening to the real accuser, Satan. He wants you stuck in guilt and shame. Jesus wants you free.

2. *Don't give in to hopeless thinking.*

Ever feel like giving up? Do you wonder if you'll complete the purpose for which God placed you on this earth? Resist despair no matter how badly you feel about yourself. This is a journey God wants you to finish. Let this promise encourage you: *He will complete the good work He started in you!*

Discouragement comes easily at times. Our natural tendency is to complain and grumble when things don't go our way. Who had a more legitimate reason to complain than Job? Maybe Joseph? These two men are examples to us of how faith in God allows us to supercede our circumstances. It's a matter of placing our priorities on God's Word, abandoning our own feelings and exercising total trust in our heavenly Father that He really will work all things together for our good.

Philippians 2:13–14 tells us that God works in us for His good pleasure, but that we are to do all things without complaining and disputing. He wants us to have all His promises, including a God image, but we can block the process. How? By grumbling and complaining, which are signs of doubt and unbelief.

If God is at work in you, hold on to His

Word and be encouraged. Nothing worthwhile is accomplished without facing a few obstacles along the way. When you meet difficulty, stand fast on God's Word, no matter how overwhelming the odds may look. God says He is faithful and will complete His good work in you. (See 1 Corinthians 10:13; Philippians 1:6.) Trust that promise.

It doesn't matter how dysfunctional your childhood was or how awful your current situation. If you trust God to complete what He has started in you, He will. Years of criticism and negative judgment can be overcome by the cross. Invite God in the process with you. Let Him fulfill His Word.

We walk by faith and not sight. You may *feel* discouraged about your life, but don't give in to that feeling. Put your trust in Him, and ask for a true picture of yourself. God wants to heal this image-struggle. He will finish what He started.

Think about the children of Israel, God's chosen people. God miraculously intervened in their lives, freed them from slavery, parted the Red Sea and provided manna daily. You know the story. Yet their response to the first sign of difficulty was to grumble and complain. Be honest; many of us do the same thing. When something goes wrong, we are quick to doubt God and let go of His Word. We tell ourselves we are stupid, no good, unable to cope and other self-deprecating comments.

The lesson to learn here is that grumbling and complaining led them to wander in the wilderness for forty more years and even prevented them from entering the Promised Land. If you feel you are wandering in a spiritual and emotional desert, stop complaining about your life. Walk by faith—not sight. Begin to praise God for who He is; then stand on His promises.

3. Accept what can't be changed.

Emotional healing begins when we accept the fact that certain things can't be changed. One of those is your genetic makeup. For example, if you feel unattractive because you have short legs, wishing you had long legs won't change anything. So accept the things you can't change, and stop wishing you were someone else.

You do, however, have control over how well you take care of the body you were given. And since your body is the temple of the Holy Spirit, eating right, getting exercise and providing self-care are important. Find a balance. Take care of yourself rather than obsess on yourself. Wishing you were thinner, smarter or more beautiful is a waste of time and energy. The goal is to be your best without engaging in idolatry of the body.

4. Engage in a realistic self-appraisal.

When I ask people to give me a list of their strengths and weaknesses, typically they provide a long list of negatives with few, if any, positives. Most of the negatives relate to outward appearance and external measures of success. Very few write down character traits or their unique gifts. So, try the following exercise:

Make a list of positive and negative statements about yourself. Include not only those things related to appearance but also how you relate to others, your personality, moral values and behavior, work or school, sports, fine arts, intelligence, service to others, spiritual intimacy and so forth.

Make the statements as factual as possible. Try not to exaggerate or overgeneralize. And don't make judgments. Instead, just describe traits and behaviors.

For example, instead of writing, "I'm fat," write, "I'm ten pounds over my ideal weight for my height." (Check a weight chart to make sure you aren't distorting this!)

Now add two columns off to the side: "Can Change" and "Can't Change." Review each item on the list, and put a check mark under "Can Change" or "Can't Change."

Finally, assign a value from 0–10 to each item on your list: 0 means it is totally unimportant, and 10 means it's of the highest importance. For example, serving others (8) may be more highly valued than having straight teeth (2).

As you review your values, notice what you give importance to—is it appearance and external things, or is it things related to kingdom values such as serving others, having compassion, being forgiving, showing kindness to others or developing patience? You may need to reprioritize based on what God values.

If your list contains items that can be changed, choose one on which to start working. Attaining personal goals helps change a negative image. For example, if you list, "I am impatient with other people and want my way," this is something you can change though prayer and interpersonal behavior. Patience is a fruit of the Spirit that grows from love.

Use the chart on page 67 for this exercise.

5. Stop comparing.

Easier said than done, right? But very important. Most people who struggle with image problems constantly compare themselves to others. Because of our individual uniqueness, it's like comparing apples and orange. Sue, for example, regularly compared her life to Ellen's.

Ellen was married to a nice guy and was expecting their first child. Ellen was raised in a very stable home with happily married parents who encouraged her. Sue, on the other hand, was the child of an alcoholic father who divorced her mother when she was ten. Sue experienced difficulty trusting people and being open. Consequently, relationships were difficult. Nonetheless, she insisted on comparing her life to Ellen's even though it depressed her. No marriage. No baby. No prospects.

Sue was setting herself up to feel failed and inferior. Her life was very different from Ellen's. She didn't recognize the truth—she wasn't a victim who couldn't overcome her past, and Ellen was not a better person. Simply comparing the two lives was an exercise in futility—they were two different people with two different lives.

We don't just confine our comparisons to friends. Often we compare ourselves to people in fashion magazines, television or movies. We forget their projected images are a result of professional makeup and hair, air brushing, computer altering, expensive wardrobes chosen by fashion experts and fabulous lighting and photography. Give me all the above, and even I could look glamorous!

Realistic Self-Appraisal			
Things I Like	Can Change	Can't Change	Value (0–10)
Straight teeth		✔	4
Things I Don't Like	Can Change	Can't Change	Value (0–10)
Don't serve others	✔		9

I once met a Ford model, one of a few fashion models selected by a top New York agency. Seeing her in the home of a friend, I would have never guessed she modeled anything. Without all the makeup, wardrobe and hair styling, she looked rather ordinary. The point is: Don't compare yourself to media images. They are not real life.

6. Lose "always" or "never" from your thinking.

My mother-in-law's premarital advice was to drop these two words from my vocabulary. Nothing happens "always" or "never." It was good advice. We all fall short of perfection, so give yourself and others a break. Paul says in Philippians 3:14 that although we are not perfect, we should concentrate on our efforts on forward motion toward what Christ has for us.

Self-degradation, self-mutilation and self-hatred are often embedded in high standards that are impossible to reach. They are also a result of the enemy's work—teaching us to destroy ourselves. You can't be perfect, and neither can others. Only Christ is sinless, so stop thinking in all-or-nothing terms and rejecting others because they fail you at times. Challenge these unrealistic thoughts, and replace them with more realistic ones. More important, ask God to speak His truth to you. His light removes the darkness.

BREAKING FREE

MENTAL HEALTH FACT

Change Your Self-Talk to God Talk

Here are examples of negative thoughts typical of someone with identity and image problems. Change this self-talk because it fuels negativity.

- *"I can't do it"* (self-doubt).
  Correction: You can't do it on your own, but with God's help, nothing is impossible. He will equip you to do what He has called you to do.

- *"I'm not liked unless I am always nice and never disagree."* (Notice the "all-or-nothing" thinking here.)
  Correction: No one feels or acts nice *all* the time. Disagreement is part of human relationships. Learn to resolve conflicts vs. avoid them.

You goal is to please only God. He loves you. Being liked by everyone else is unrealistic.

- *"I am no good."* **Correction:** Your sin nature is no good. Repent when you sin, and live in God's grace. There is no goodness apart from God. But when you become one of His, you are a new creation and covered by His blood.
- *"I should (fill in the blank), but I'm not."* **Correction:** "Shoulds" get us in trouble unless they relate to biblical instruction. For example, we *should* love our neighbor and work on doing this because God commands it. The majority of image problems, however, stem from unrealistic expectations: "I should be thin." "I should make money." Evaluate the "shoulds" to see if they are scriptural mandates that we try to achieve through the Holy Spirit in us or are ridiculous expectations we put on ourselves.
- *"If I'm not perfect, I won't be loved."* **Correction:** You are loved because God chose you. He doesn't look for perfection. He

wants you. You can make mistakes. His grace is able to handle them.

- *"I can't handle life."* **Correction:** With God's help and the support of others, you can handle what comes your way. Difficulty may come, but God promises His presence and comfort. In fact, He promises never to allow you to experience more than you and His Spirit in you can handle.
- *"I hate my body."* **Correction:** If your body has suffered from a lack of self-care, begin to take care of it. Otherwise, you hate what God designed. He's already chosen you as His bride. He wants your heart, not your physical body, but He created that body.

Strategies to Help Change Your Negative Thoughts

If you feel stuck in trying to change your thoughts and line them up with God's Word, these strategies may help:

1. *Thought stopping*

Practice what therapists call *thought stopping*. It is a practical way to renew your mind. Negative and self-destructive thoughts play on each other and often lead to depression and anxiety. Thought stopping can be used to deal with those negative thoughts. It is simple in concept, harder to apply.

When an ungodly or self-degrading thought comes into your head, interrupt your stream of thought. Silently yell "stop" and force yourself to think about something else. Or do something to startle yourself in order to stop the thought, such as pinch yourself, snap a rubber band on your wrist, get up or take a deep breath. Then refocus your thoughts on something positive (use the scriptures in the previous chapters on God esteem and identity in Christ).

If you can't seem to shake the thought, command it to stop. You have this power because of the Holy Spirit in you. Thoughts that discourage often lead to depression and feelings of hopelessness.

They are not from God, and you have the power to stop them.

2. *Challenge extreme thoughts.*

If you exaggerate, overgeneralize or engage in what's called "catastrophic" thinking (imagine the worst possible scenario), you can learn to recognize and challenge those thoughts. Ask yourself if the thought is true all the time, some of the time or once in a while. Most likely, you'll quickly see the exaggeration. Write out your exaggerated thought, and then write down an alternative, more realistic one. Modify the extreme thought by substituting the alternative.

3. *Refocus.*

When inward thoughts turn negative, try to refocus those thoughts on something or someone else. Force yourself to think about your neighbor, ways you can help others and the gifts God has given you. How can you use those gifts for His glory? Take your mind off yourself, and refocus on something or someone else.

BREAKING FREE

MENTAL HEALTH FACT

Think on Positive Things

Philippians 4:8 instructs us to think on positive things. Think about things that are true, noble, just, pure, lovely, of good report, virtuous, or anything praiseworthy. List the blessings in your life, the times of answered prayer, the testimonies of others, a kind deed, the beauty of creation and so forth. You can always find something positive on which to focus your thoughts.

Challenge your self-centered attitude. You are part of a big family—the family of God. How do you fit into the Great Commission to win others to the Lord? Are you more concerned about personal preferences, church practices and getting every need met each week at church, or are you asking God to use you to win others? Is your focus all about you, or do you think about how to advance the kingdom of God?

4. Set realistic goals.

So often people in therapy believe change should be quick and easy. Changing habits and negative thinking takes time and patience. Begin by making small changes that will move you along the path of godly living. For example, if you are disgusted with your body because you weigh 260 pounds, don't expect to diet to a size two. You may laugh, but people have these kinds of expectations. Unrealistic goals are setups for feeling failed and discouraged. A more realistic goal would be to control your eating at a given meal. A realistic weight loss goal would be to lose ten pounds and keep it off.

I've counseled people who have been delivered from drugs, depression, eating disorders and other addictions. Sometimes healing is immediate. Other times healing is progressive.

And don't panic if you stumble along the road to healing. Instead, ask what triggered the behavior. Pray, "Is there still something here to be healed?" If so, trust God to reveal it to you and move forward.

5. Sit in His presence.

If you struggle with accepting God's view of you, then get out your Bible and read the specific scriptures outlined in chapter three. Read those scriptures over and over until they penetrate your thoughts. Pray and worship God. As you worship and love God, He will give you a revelation of His love for you. Sitting in His presence will change you. The more intimate you are with God, the more you will directly experience His love. It will heal you.

BREAKING FREE

PRAYER FOR YOU

Lord, help me to renew my mind daily. I will hide Your Word in my heart and line up my thoughts with Yours. Help me see when and where my thinking strays so that I can correct those thoughts.

CHAPTER 5

BREAK-FREE STRATEGIES: CHANGE YOUR BEHAVIOR

If you keep doing what you've always done, you'll keep getting what you've always got.

—PETER FRANCISCO

Not only do we need to renew our minds daily, but new action may also be needed. Here are twenty-one action strategies to help you break free from negative self-image.

1. *Start using your gifts.*

God has uniquely gifted you. You don't have to be a pastor or worship leader to use your gifts. Don't hide your talent in the ground or, in the other extreme, boast in pride. Stir up those gifts and use them for His glory.

2. Take responsibility for your life.

Don't blame your looks, family, people or anything else for your problems. Instead make a choice to start behaving differently. When you become a child of God, you are no longer a victim. His Spirit empowers you to do great things in His name no matter what your background. In fact, He often uses the lowly to do great things. Take responsibility and act like royalty. You are His child and have inherited much. You can change with the help of the Holy Spirit.

3. List positive things you can do with your time.

Don't obsess on your appearance or be driven by success. Serve others by taking a meal, repairing something broken, baby-sitting a child, offering to drive. Or spend time in quiet contemplation by reading, taking walks, going to a museum, listening to music. Find new interests and hobbies.

4. Develop a support system of people who love and care about you.

One way to help correct a negative image is to surround yourself with people who will be honest and open with you but love you no matter what. As you trust trustworthy people, you learn that love is not contingent on what you do or how you look.

5. Avoid or spend less time with those who are critical and judgmental of appearance and abilities.

It's hard to stay focused on the importance of godly character when constantly surrounded by those whose focus is on outward appearances and material things. Find friends who care about kingdom values and who won't play the comparison game.

6. Improve your relationships with others.

The better you relate to others and serve them, the better you will feel about yourself. As you become less self-focused and more others-focused, your image problems will fade. When you show love in tangible ways, you are following the command of Jesus. Don't wait for others to become loving. Love them with God's love first. Become a better listener; have more compassion and empathy. These skills improve relationships.

7. *Read and listen to stories of people who triumphed over difficulty.*

When you hear a story about overcoming incredible odds, it gives hope. For example, read the story of Abe Lincoln. He failed twice in business, and he lost an election, his mother (early in life), his father, a lover and a child. He also lost other appointments and elections before becoming president. In addition, he struggled with severe depression. Yet, he handled his defeats and was an example of a humble, sensitive and great president. Listen to people who didn't give up and who trusted God through difficulty. The Bible is full of these stories. They are there to encourage you. Let them.

8. *Don't wait to look perfect.*

So many people stop engaging in life because they don't feel good about themselves. In therapy, they say, "I'll do ___ when I lose weight." Or, "I'll call a friend when I feel better about myself." Don't wait; you'll feel more isolated and upset. Take a step now; start reconnecting with friends and become active.

9. Ask friends what they find attractive.

Those of you really stuck in negative self-image may want to ask friends what they find attractive. Their answers may surprise you. The purpose of this exercise isn't to base your life on their opinions, but to become more aware of how narrow your thinking may be. For example, women are often surprised to hear that male friends don't find ultra-thin women attractive.

10. Make exercise enjoyable.

When you exercise because of guilt or compulsion, you have a problem. If you feel addicted to exercise, find something enjoyable that is active but not compulsive. For example, instead of running five miles every day and feeling upset if you miss a day, try rollerblading or playing tennis for fun! Choose an enjoyable activity that allows you to interact with others. If you are unable to break out of a compulsive routine, you may need to see a counselor.

11. Learn to say no.

You aren't loved because you do things for others. If you are, then the relationship is built on the wrong foundation. Learn to say *no* and be assertive.

12. Pray and stay intimate with God.

We all want to belong to someone or something bigger than ourselves. Make time to be a friend of God. You belong to Him.

13. Be open to the plan of God for your life.

It is important to develop goals and make plans, but do so in consultation with God. He will lead and direct your steps if you include Him in the process. Keep a journal that tracks your progress and answers to prayer as a way to stay focused and encouraged.

14. Live a biblical life.

Imitate Christ. The Bible is clear about obedience and how it relates to blessing.

15. Be outraged at media.

Speak up about the negative effects

media have on women and girls. Write letters to editors of magazines and tell them you've had enough. Talk to your children about what they see and how it relates to God's acceptance of us. Resist stereotypes.

16. Listen to your daughters as they talk about their bodies and unrealistically compare them to the Barbie dolls in their rooms.

Correct their thinking to a healthier view of the female body. Barbie isn't the best image. Who looks like this doll? Provide other role models.

17. Resist the culture of thinness and dieting.

Don't abuse your body with fad diets and weight-loss gimmicks. Develop good eating habits and nutrition. It's good to exercise and take care of your body. Just don't go to extremes and make the body an idol or the constant object of focus.

18. Throw away your scales.

If you obsess about weight, get rid of the scales or stay off them. If your mood is dependent on how much you weigh any given day, seek help from a counselor. Work on the total person now. Find your worth from God, not a number on the scale.

19. Don't fall in love with products that promise happiness.

Only a relationship with God brings true happiness. There is no magic product or pill. Do you recall the TV sweater commercial that said (I'm paraphrasing here), "The boyfriend may leave, but your sweater will always be with you"? The message is that you can't count on people, but you can on things. Wrong! Count on God.

20. Talk character, not physical appearances.

With so much cultural obsession on bodies and glamour, talk about the *character* of people rather than their looks. Teens with eating disorders often have parents who emphasize appearance and presenting a good image to others.

21. Value the things God values. Live out those values.

Develop a biblical world-view and live your life accordingly. How do you determine the value of something? Value is determined by how much you pay for it. Jesus bought you with a price—His life. Obviously He places great value on you.

BREAKING FREE

PRAYER FOR YOU

Lord, it is my desire to imitate Christ. Forgive me when I fail to obey Your Word. Help me take a stand for righteousness. Change my heart and actions so they align with Your Word. Above all, fill me with Your love so I can effectively love others and be less self occupied.

CHAPTER 6

BREAKING FREE SUMMARY

The more we get what we now call "ourselves" out of the way and let Him take over, the more truly ourselves we become.

—C. S. LEWIS

Have you embraced a distorted view of yourself? Have you used the cultural standards of beauty and success to judge your worth? For the Christian, there is no such thing as self-image. We are made in God's image to reflect His glory.

Christian self-evaluation is done as an act of responsibility. The Bible tells us how to think of ourselves and how to act. Jesus challenges us to be more like Him and less like our human nature. We understand that we are all sinners in need of redemption.

When you contrast this to the secular,

stark differences are apparent. Modern views of the *self* are based on the idea that each person decides what is right and should know himself or herself well enough to determine the course of action for his or her life. This is called *self-reliance*. But we are not self-reliant; we need divine guidance to accomplish the purposes for our existences. The more we try to live apart from God, the more we fail.

Remember we are never truly our own. As C. S. Lewis points out: "The more I resist Him and try to live on my own, the more I become dominated by my own heredity and upbringing and surroundings and natural desires. In fact, what I so proudly call 'Myself' becomes merely the meeting place for trains of events which I never started and I cannot stop."[1]

Break Free to His Image

God invites us to a personal relationship in which we can find ultimate acceptance. With His help, we can break free from a negative self-image. Review these points in order to correct your image.

1. Have a proper understanding of what self-image is.

A *self*-image is based on your own ideas of acceptance and accomplishment. It is highly influenced by the culture and values around you. A *God* image is built on the inherent dignity and worth you have as His child. Because you were created by Him and reflect His image, nothing you do or accomplish impacts your worth. God chose you (chapter one).

2. God esteems you when people do not.

God cares about your heart and looks to things of eternal significance. People look on the outward appearance. Worth is often judged by looks, success and accomplishments. Scripture reminds us that we are accepted, secure and significant because we are His. Read the scriptures outlined for a better understanding of how you are a reflection of God (chapter two).

3. At the root of a negative self-image is a lack of true identity.

If identity is based on anything other than who we are in Christ, it can be shattered.

Identity in Christ is necessary to develop God esteem. No matter what your past, salvation changes you to a new creation and immediately connects you to the family of God. He desires you, a son or daughter of royalty, to act like His child and reflect His image (chapter three).

4. Daily renew your mind with the Word of God.

Value what God does. Change begins in your thought life. As you think on things that are good, pure, noble, lovely and of good report, review the promises of God. Identify the lies of the enemy and ask God to reveal His truth about who you are. You will be at peace (chapter four).

5. Change your behavior.

If we engage in cultural prescriptions to build self-esteem, we will fail. There is never enough we can do to improve. And we will always fall short. So stop striving for self-actualization and ways to be loved. Obey His Word, and you will receive His blessings. Rest in Him and allow His love to transform you (chapter five).

FINAL THOUGHTS

THE HOPE

Deception is Satan's game. If he can deceive you into thinking you have a *self* apart from God, he will. He doesn't want you to know your true identity and hates that you were created in the image of God. If he can convince you to stop believing the truth, he has a chance to destroy you. The last thing he wants you to do is reflect God's image.

So he tries to trick you into believing false views of the self. If he is successful, you'll develop an eating disorder, depression or anxiety. Your shaky and ungrounded sense of self will lead to dissatisfaction and breakdown. Or perhaps he'll convince you that esteem is based on the attainment of power, success, influence or sexuality. It's an age-old seduction—see that forbidden tree, go ahead and eat it, and you'll be like God.

When you fall short in performing (we

all do), he says, "See, I told you. You can't be good enough for God, so give it up." And he's hoping you will become discouraged and give up. Then you'll turn your attention to the false images of self that appear attainable—a beautiful body, wealth, fame, materialism and hedonism.

Jesus knows Satan's game plan. And in Luke 10:38–42, He addresses our temptation to be caught up in anything that distracts from Him—the truth and the way. Remember the story of Mary and Martha? Jesus comes to visit. I mean, can you imagine? Jesus is coming to your house! I have to admit, I'd be a lot more like Martha than Mary. Everything would have to be just right—clean, cook and serve His every need. Sound familiar?

When He came to the door, Martha moves into action—serve Him. She was focused on *doing* for Jesus, not on the *person* of Jesus. And when her sister didn't join her in her serving frenzy, she got upset. "How dare Mary sit at His feet and let me do all the work."

Mary was doing something, but Martha

couldn't see it. She was at the feet of Jesus, enjoying His presence. Jesus responds by telling both sisters that Mary, the listener, has "chosen what is better." This was not a put-down of Martha's efforts. And Jesus wasn't comparing the sisters and saying, "I like Mary better." He used the occasion to teach Martha what was important—being distracted by work or "performing" is not what He wants from us. Being with Him, listening to Him is what He desires. He knows that when we sit at His feet, we feel loved and esteemed.

This brief biblical account is a reminder not to become distracted by the things of this world that have no eternal significance—beautifying the body, making money, seeking fame and success. None of these things will improve our image in God's eyes. We don't impress Him with our efforts. He only wants us to return the love and affection He has for us.

Don't get caught up in the lie of building self-esteem. You are already esteemed because you are a child of God. Sit at His feet. Obey His Word, and be transformed by His love. Your worth comes from God, no other source. Break free from a negative self-image. You are His bride, chosen, loved and esteemed.

BREAKING FREE

PRAYER FOR YOU

Lord, I give You all my performance efforts and striving in my own power in order to be good enough for You. Forgive me. Right now, I want to choose the best part—to sit at Your feet and be Your friend. Your love will transform me. Help me be less distracted by the culture that presents false ways to build esteem. Thank You for esteeming me and making me a beautiful reflection of You. Amen.

NOTES

CHAPTER 1

1. A. E. Field, L. Cheung, A. M. Wolf, D. B. Herzog, S. L. Gortmaker and G. A. Colditz, "Exposure to the mass media and weight concerns among girls," *Pediatrics*: 103(3) (March 1999): E36.
2. Wells, Bednar & Peterson, *Self-esteem: Paradoxes and Innovations in Clinical Theory and Practice* (Washington, DC: American Psychological Association, 1989).
3. S. Harter, "Developmental perspectives on the self system," In E.M. Hetherington (Ed.), *Socialization, Personality, and Social Development*, Vol. 4 of P. Mussen (Ed.) *Handbook of Child Psychology*. Fourth Edition (New York: J. Wiley, 1983).
4. R. M. Kowalski, "Half-Baked Idea: Patriotic Fervor in the Aftermath of Operation Desert Storm: Basking in Reflected Glory?" *Contemporary Social Psychology* 15(4) (1991): 118–120.
5. J. Leo, "Damn, I'm Good," *U.S. News* Online, 1998. Retrieved 8-10-2001: www.usnews.com/usnews/issue/980518/18john.htm.
6. S. Parker, M. Nichter, N. Nichter, N. Vuckovic, C. Sims and C. Ritenbaugh,

"Body image and weight concerns among African-American and white adolescent females: Differences that make a difference," *Human Organization* 54 (1995): 103–114.
7. J. Leo, "Damn, I'm good!" Retrieved online 8-10-2001: www.usnews.com/usnews/issue/980518/18john.htm.
8. E. Staub, "Aggression and self-esteem," *The APA Monitor* online, 1999. Retrieved 8-10-01: www.apa.org/monitor/jan99/point.html.
9. L. G. Katz, "Self-Esteem and Narcissism: Implications for practice," *ERIC Digest*, 1993. Retrieved online 3-30-02: www.ed.gov/databases/ERIC_Digests/ed358973.html.
10. Well-connected report: Weight and diet. *Who becomes obese or overweight?* Retrieved online 4-8-02: www.webmd.com/content/article/1689.52905.
11. "Eating disorder in the USA: Statistics in context." Retrieved online 4-8-02: www.edap.org/edinfo/stats.html.
12. "Eating disorder in the USA: Statistics in context." Retrieved online 4-8-02: www.edap.org/edinfo/stats.html.

Chapter 3

1. Os Guinness, *The Call* (Nashville: Word Publishing, 1998).
2. James Langteax, *God.com* (Sisters, OR: Multnomah Publishers, 2000), 15.
3. Oswald Chambers, *My Utmost for His Highest* (New York: Dodd, Mead & Company, 1935), 7.
4. Ibid.
5. Freedom in Christ Ministries has graciously given permission to adapt these statements from their "Who I Am in Christ" statements found on their ministry website www.ficm.org, originally written by Neil T. Anderson, copyright © Freedom in Christ.

Chapter 6

1. C. S. Lewis quote taken from Guinness, *The Call*, 25.